Unrationed Hope

poems

Judith Duvall

Iris Press
Oak Ridge, Tennessee

Book design: Robert B. Cumming, Jr.

Library of Congress Cataloging-in-Publication Data

Names: Duvall, Judith, 1938- author.
Title: Unrationed hope : poems / Judith Duvall.
Description: Oak Ridge, Tennessee : Iris Press, 2016.
Identifiers: LCCN 2016008131 | ISBN 9781604542387
(pbk. : alk. paper)
Subjects: LCSH: World War, 1939-1945—Poetry.
Classification: LCC PS3604.U823 A6 2016 | DDC 811/.6—dc23
LC record available at https://lccn.loc.gov/2016008131

Acknowledgments

My first and deepest gratitude goes to my editor and friend, Cathy Kodra, who, along with Bob Cumming of Iris Press, lent encouragement and mentoring throughout the creation of this project. I appreciate the members of the Knoxville Writers' Guild Advanced Poetry Group who patiently reviewed many of these poems.

A very special thank you to my friend of many years, artist Janet Browning. Her skillful illustrations give the reader another look into the daily lives of Americans during the WWII era.

Thanks to family members who never wavered in their support: my sister Janice Emge, my children Rick Allen and Karla, Cyndi Randall and Gary; and Tim Allen and Lisa. My grandchildren, Jamie and Jordan Randall always expressed their belief in my work, as did Hannah, Brooke, and Riley Allen.

Gratitude to friends Scott Savage, Peggy Douglas, Rebecca Council, Martha Yarnell, Joan MacReynolds; also Vickie Jordan, Diana Cruze, and Judy Blackstock, who read poems and gave encouragement.

In addition, I extend heartfelt thanks to all those I have not named here who have crossed my path and lent encouragement and insight to this undertaking. Special thanks to our World War II veterans, both those who served in active duty abroad and those who served in myriad ways at home.

I dedicate these poems to the men and women who fought on the battlefields of WWII, and to the citizens who kept America united, strong, and ready for their victorious return. Thank you.

In no direction that we turn do we find ease or comfort. If we are honest and if we have the will to win we find only danger, hard work and iron resolution.

—Wendell Willkie, *Work, Win, Turn*

Contents

I.

II.

III.

Author Note

The first poem in this collection came about during a meeting of a poetry-writing group of the Knoxville Writers' Guild. After I read my poem, some members of the group encouraged me to pursue the idea of writing more poems about the WWII era. Surprised at the idea, but encouraged by their approval, I began to read and research events of those years, and then, surprisingly, I began to remember some relevant events from my own early childhood years.

One of the first memories was at my grandparents' house with the adults of the family listening in solemn silence to radio evening news. From my view tucked behind my grandfather's chair, it seemed a lot like church. Later, when my uncles and cousins had gone off to war, I spent many hours with my grandmother. I watched her bustling around her kitchen, helped her gather vegetables from the garden, and enjoyed the magic of her canning kitchen. No matter what we were doing, she talked to me with simple candor about the family and answered my questions about the war. I do not remember ever being afraid, but I was much older before I realized that life did not have to be so serious and sad.

Those memories, along with interviews with people who survived the times and / or had family who did, provide the ideas for the stories I tell with these poems.

As I wrote these poems, it became increasingly clear to me that those of us who live in the United States today are here because seven decades ago, brave and determined people made sacrifices. Men and women, teens and children did not hesitate to do whatever it took to keep their country working and united in the face of the most horrible threat anyone had ever known.

The country in which I write this today is different from that time, and the freedom that allowed these changes to evolve is intact through the faith, hard work, and determination of those who kept this country ready for the return of those fighting on the war fronts.

As you read these poems, I hope the stories of the men, women, teens, and children will convey the hopes, hardships, loves, and losses they endured for their steadfast belief in victory.

—Judith Duvall

I. Letters

Our eyes devour the words...

Sweethearts and Wives

Each day we walk to the mailbox,
open it, breathless, pulsebeat
in our ears. Relief, joy
when we find an envelope,
stripe-edged in red, blue,
transparent sheets folded inside.
Words—blue-inked loops, spikes
suspended
across the pages like water lilies
on a clear pond.

Our eyes devour the words,
their meaning gives a vision
of his face
whiskered, smudged with the dirt
of battle. We feel the caress of
a finger down our cheek, the brush
of lips against our hair, and passion
slips from the page, whispers in our ear.

We brush the letters with our lips,
breathe, hoping for the scent
of a memory.
We hold the pages against our heart,
let waves of desire take us to a place
that transcends
all thoughts of war.

Letters from the Armory

The child listens intently to every word
penned by the favorite aunt whose bright
hair and swishy skirts caused church lady
whispers. Word came that she rode the train

to Baltimore to work in an armory;
we shed lonely tears. No more silk stockings,
perfumed hankies, lacy underwear piled
on the spare room bed. No more stories

of fashion shows, high heels, fancy
shopping sprees. No more whispered
tales of night clubs, taxicabs, all-night
dancing with handsome men in uniform.

Mama's tender voice reads some lines
over and over. She, like the child, cannot
picture dainty hands that never pulled a weed,
scrubbed a pan, clad in rough gloves pushing

great mounds of metal into furnaces, guiding
the molten spew into gun molds bound for war.
Coveralls her uniform, a kerchief hides blond
curls, stiff boots stride treacherous aisles.

Her boss, a woman from Wisconsin, never
tires, smiles, or understands auntie's little
jokes, her tinkling laugh or southern drawl.

The Letter

The letter said battle wounds,
he'll be sent home. We clasped hands,
murmured hope, fought back tears.

Fear rose,
bile in our throats, swallowed down,
as long-silent words rushed out,
rasping sounds of a faith held fast.

The wounds don't matter,
our dear boy is coming home.

Ghost Life

Slumped against the sill, she
stares out the upstairs window, one
hand clutching a velvet box,

the other a crumpled note. Dressing
gown rumpled, once-golden curls
hanging limp. The brothers

watch from the doorway, wonder
what keeps her apart from them,
content in loneliness. Perhaps

the crime of trust, passion for a soldier
who warmed her bed, poured love
songs into her heart. They never knew

him or when he was here. She kept
the secret, his words the mystery
that locks her in this room.

Weekly Letters, 1943

Every week the letters come,
words choked with steel, noise,
molten gun metal.
She calls her new friends *sisters*,
works men's work—
lifts, shoves, slams,
pushes heavy carts through treacherous aisles.

The children's minds jumble
thinking of their pretty aunt's
blond curls bound in course kerchiefs,
fancy skirt replaced with coveralls,
painted nails hidden in asbestos gloves,
long eyelashes singed in a Baltimore armory.

Handsome fly-boy groom
flies deadly missions over dark waters,
dreams of his bride wearing lace,
hair perfumed, lips parted in passion,
eager for his return.

Week after week the letters come;
Mama's voice caresses every word.
The children listen, willing her sweet syllables
to soften the foreign sounds of war.

For When the Boys Come Home

I find her on the porch, hands
limp in a bowl of snap beans,
staring at the back yard, lost
in shadows I cannot see.

Mama's waiting for the beans,
unheard, hollow words fall
on sister's melancholy soul.
New husband, baby brother

both gone to war, both owning
her heart. *You hear me, Jessie?*
Mama needs the beans. Eyelids
flicker, tears slide down pale

cheeks. Hands worn beyond
her years return to the chore.
She rocks back and forth,
breaks a bean, voice quivers:

Tell Mama we'll need to can extra
for when the boys come home.

Mama's in the kitchen scalding
jars, tight lipped and quiet,
yellow telegram poking
from an apron pocket.

USO Promise

When the train pulls in from Jersey,
word spreads fast. Marilou Marzetti
is back in town with lots of news,
at last, at last.

Clickety clack, clickety clack
our friend is back, chitter and chat.
Girls from high school, girls from the mill
all gather to hear:

They were sweet boys, short boys, tall boys,
scared, yet brave. Oh, we danced and danced,
never talked of war. *You are so pretty, will*
you write to me? send photographs?
Promise me, honey, say you will.
Oh, I did, girls, I did.

Clickety clack, clickety clack
Marilou's back, chitter and chat.
Girls from high school, girls from the mill
news is good, nice to hear:

I have lots of names—you girls help me,
take one, or two, or more. Write friendly letters,
send photos, happy news, and keep on writing
until—well—keep on writing.

Chitter and chat, chitter and chat.
Girls from high school, girls from the mill
smile and wonder,
will they write back?

Scraps of paper flutter across the soda shop
counter, brave boys, scared boys, sailors,
soldiers, fly boys, and Marines; all gone to war
holding a tiny dream, a USO girl's promise.

Chitter and chat, chitter and chat.
Girls from high school, girls from the mill
grasp the names,
vow they'll write—until.

Brave Faith

Kathryn Gray clocks in at Stringer's
Market every morning at seven, dons
her brown work smock, readies her
cash register for the day's business.

Her voice is friendly, customers love
her, she smiles, has a kind word for all.
Mr. Stringer says he couldn't run
the store without her.

She leaves the store, walks seven
blocks to a small house with green
shutters. 33 Maple Street, *Our*
lucky number, Larry said.

She dines alone most nights,
Sundays she takes turns having
pot roast with her folks, fried
chicken with Larry's mom and dad.

Her life seems normal, good
for an American soldier's wife
during the worst time in world
history. Last May, she received

news that Larry was missing
in action. She won't believe he's
gone, just missing. He'll come back
to their lucky-number home.

Each night Kathryn lights a candle,
says prayers. She opens a box, unties
a blue ribbon, and begins to read
letters from her beloved.

Dear Aunt Margaret,

Betty Sue Johnson took me
to the picture show last week.
I argued against it pretty strong,
but she insisted we needed
time off from wringing our hands
over soldiers at war and wondering
what awful thing we'll hear
on the radio news tonight.

She said we should wear our church
clothes, dress up, try to feel festive.
(Betty Sue likes to use words like festive.)
We haven't had a single party of any
kind for two years, and we deserve
some fun, even if it is just a movie.
She said she missed Joey (her fella)
as much as anyone missed their
soldier man but couldn't see how
it helped him or the war effort for her
to mope around feeling guilty
for simply being alive.

I was surprised at how many people
were at the picture show that night.
We didn't have extra nickels for
popcorn, but we brought a few pieces
of hard candy saved from Christmas.
We were already licking our fingers
when the lights dimmed and the music
began. The first thing was the previews,
and I can tell you there's some shows
coming that'll be something to see.
Girls in fancy dresses singing and dancing
up and down sparkly stairs. Why, I'd

be plumb out of breath just one time
up and down them steps, couldn't
breathe, let alone sing.

There's another show coming that's
about a woman who is trying to find
out who killed her boyfriend. She has
the blondest hair I ever seen.
A cowboy show is coming too, but I didn't
quite understand them cowboys talking
about chasing outlaws, then the next
minute they're riding slow-like and
singing to a girl riding a horse next
to 'em. There was a few more previews
with fancy dancing girls and sorry-lookin'
guys that drank too much. I had to keep
reminding myself it was just pretend
stuff so I wouldn't feel sorry for the girls
that got their hearts broke and the poor
men who couldn't hold their likker.

Well, Aunt Margaret, after the previews
(the poster out front calls them coming
attractions), came the newsreels. That's
what it says—"News Reels"—sounds like
fishing gear don't it, but anyway, here
it came. The loudest music you ever heard
in your life came blaring out and made
me and Betty Sue jump. We giggled
at ourselves, but that sure didn't last
long. Soon we was seeing our poor
wounded soldiers, blood everywhere,
faces so tired you knew they was
numb. I guess you know all about
it, so I'll stop now. This war's awful,
and like me and the rest of the family,

I know you pray for it to end.

Your Niece,
Joanie

II. Home

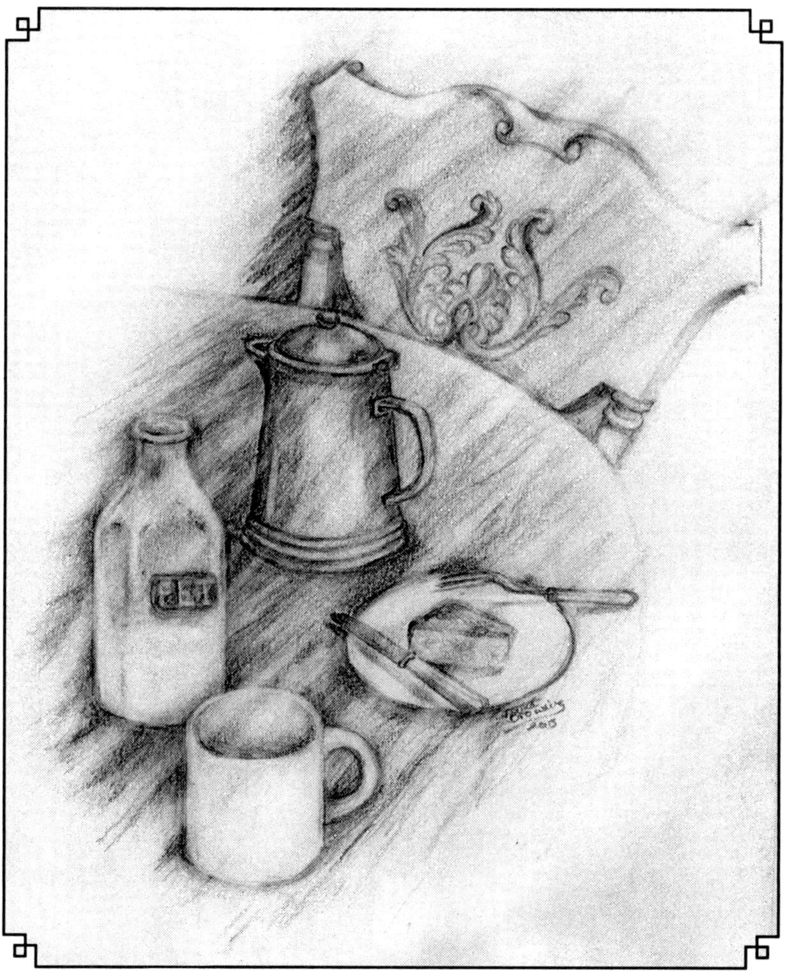

simple thanks for beans, cornbread...

Winter 1941

My Papa sat in his armchair,
reading the newspaper,
smoking Lucky Strikes.

He was so grouchy
no one dared talk to him;
he'd just pick a fight.

He went on and on: *Europe needs*
to fight their own war. It was the
only time he agreed with Roosevelt.

Then
the Japs
bombed Pearl Harbor.

We declared war,
and everything
changed.

Three of my brothers
signed up and were gone
by January.

The one with the bad knee
goes to work every day
at the bank.

Mama stays busy
in the kitchen,
tries not to be sad.

Papa sits in his armchair,
reading the newspaper,
smoking Lucky Strikes.

Kitchen Patriot

Cliffs of Dover on a map
brings a vision of Mama
stirring and fussing
at the kitchen stove,
singing along with the radio,
"There'll be blue birds over
the White Cliffs of Dover,"
waving her spoon, wrinkling
her brow,
clucking her tongue
and tsking over
our poor boys, their torment
and suffering, the maniacal deeds
that brought us into the war.

If I could just go to Washington
and talk with Mr. Roosevelt,
she anguished,
flinging an apron over her face
to hide the welling tears.

Nights of Waiting

I sit alone at the kitchen table
listening to the loud, slow ticking of the clock,
seeing only dark shapes in the stillness of night.
The scenes in my head are bloody, vivid.

Listening to the loud, slow ticking of the clock.
I think of how the war controls our lives.
The scenes in my head are bloody, vivid.
I cannot escape the images, the fear.

I think how the war controls our lives.
When I sleep, my dreams are battlefields.
I cannot escape the images, the fear.
I leave my bed, sit quietly in the dark.

If I sleep, I dream of battlefields.
I wake soaked with sweat, trembling, afraid.
I leave my bed, smoke cigarettes in the cold.
Smoke settles around me like a bad idea.

I wake soaked in sweat, trembling, afraid.
My son, my boy is fighting deep in France,
where smoke and dust settle like a bad idea.
Is my boy safe? Is he afraid?

My son is fighting a battle in France.
I see only a little hope in the pre-dawn light.
Is my boy safe? I believe he is afraid.
I sit at the kitchen table alone.

Dedicated Needles

She rocks, murmurs
ancient ballads
leached from the pain
of blue and gray,
men who swore,
boys who prayed.

Clicking worn steel,
her needles move
in dream cadence
knitting rows
of hope, chains
of chance, each stitch

a lost embrace,
each purl a pause in time
marching on frozen
sod, where bleeding feet
clad in cracked battle boots
ache for soft wool.

Dog Days

Summer's here. Granny says dog days
mean laziness, humidity, and garden weeds
thrive. Mama's ordered pears picked;
I'm assigned the chore.

I'm on the back steps, bucket
ready, shoes tied, yellowjackets eyeing
me from the yard. Horrid stinging beasts,
buzzing over the windfalls.

Raymond gathered pears last summer,
his chore since a boy. We don't talk
about Raymond—the war, killing, wounded
—unless a neighbor comes to visit.

We came home early from the watermelon
feast 'cause Mr. Hollins kept talking 'bout
his son, crippled for life, missing a leg. Mama
cried, wringing her hands,
Lord, keep Raymond safe, bring him home
to us the same sweet boy we sent off to war.

The Harvest

Plump roasting ears peek out the crib,
firm turnips and 'taters safe in the cellar.
Shiny jars of beans and 'maters, red
and green as Christmas, shelved and cool
after the sweat of harvest. Hickory,

oak, and a bit of pine stacked high
bulge the woodshed. Abundance
of life and labor fills heart and home,
but nothing fills the emptiness
of Jeb's place at the table

or erases the echo of his laughter,
his soft, sweet voice—*Thankee kindly*
for that good dinner, Mama—
as he heads to the barn for chores
or leaves to fight The War.

Sacrifices

I found him in the back yard
sitting on a rickety old bench
smoking his pipe. He gave no
hint of my presence until
he pointed to the license
plates hanging on the toolshed
wall. They were lined in order
of years, he explained, of cars
he'd bought and sold.

I noted the one dated two years
before my brother Terry was born.

It was a 1936 Chevrolet Master
Deluxe; I paid five hundred eighty
dollars for it, and traded it for
the coupe we have now.

I waited for more, but he took his
hammer and began pulling nails,
removing the plates one by one.
When he stepped away, there was
one plate left, and shadowed outlines
of those removed.

I'm leaving that one, the year
we went to war. I'll take it down
when your dad comes home.

I carried the stack of plates to the
curb, dropped them into the scrap metal
collection box. Grandpa remained on
the bench, turned away from
the lone plate with its rust-edged
numbers, 1941.

Grandpa's Sword

From under the bed he brings his ancient treasure,
unwraps a faded scarf, spits on a rag, begins to polish.

With careful strokes he tells of enemies fought, buddies
felled, stories they shared—victories won, blood spilled.

The children watch, cautious fingers touching the gleaming
blade, entranced by the glimpse of gore its sharp edge dreams.

The radio blares news of planes, bombs, casualties in lands
foreign to his ear. New battles he cannot fathom.

Kitchen Table

We read our stories in scars,
scratches, a scorch here and there.
Our lives recorded in good
times, sad times, fits of anger,
times of tears; ink stains witness
small sweaty hands grasping
pens, scratching grade-school homework.

Here were birthday parties, plant
promotions. Graduation
time came for Alice: small gifts,
no sugar rations for cake,
simple thanks for beans, cornbread.
Our proud girl burst into song:
Happy days are here again.

We tried to believe her smile
while we struggled not to stare
at the deep gouge left where Mike
tried whittling with a paring knife.
He was nine, ten years ago,
before he knew a bayonet.

Altar Call, 1944

More prompt than a priestly
summons to mass
or scheduled Sunday sermon,
the altar call comes each night
at six.

The faithful family
sinks into doily adorned mohair
like storm-weary warriors
oblivious to snowflakes
on spilled blood.

Clutching faded afghans,
twisting apron hems,
smoking cigarettes,
they listen
in holy silence.

The oak-veneered Philco
spews the commentator's
rasping dirge:

The Battle Casualties of the Day.

Home Safe

Dad leans against the doorjamb,
listening to muffled moans
coming from Terry's room.
Tears flowing, he thinks:
My boy is home safe, alive,
but his mind is trapped by
the prison bars of evil.

Mom listens from her pillow,
feels the pain of helplessness
to take away the horror dreams
her son relives every night.
She thinks:
He's safe from bullets,
but not The War.

At breakfast they exchange
looks: *What are we to do?*

Homecoming Feast

Steamy windows witness
simmering vegetables bubbling, delectable
promise of garden-grown beans, corn, yams.
The child, flour-sack bibbed, washed, perched on a stool,
grandmother's eager helper pulls
tender meat, tiny fingers probe
hidden morsels, the hen a war-time luxury.
Rolling pin magic spreads creamy white pillows,
the child cuts dumplings, biscuits.
Root cellar apples, peeled, chopped;
pie crust latticed, into the oven.
A stack cake reigns over jars that sparkle
deep purple, reds, oranges of homemade jams,
verdant pickles, multi-colored relish.
The child asks, *Are we having a feast?*
A smile, a tear on a flour-smudged cheek:
Yes, our boys are coming home.

The Piano

For my sister, Janice Marie

Scary war talk and a whiny grandchild pushed
Grandma out the door to prowl penniless among
the treasures of Amos Pritchard's secondhand store.
There she conjured up magic that put a piano
in the parlor. She insisted the old upright sit
next to Grandpa's easy chair, his amber ashtray
overflowing its metal stand. He grumped, growled,
winked at Janice Marie. On Sunday, Amos Pritchard's
bony knees crowded under our dinner table.

More magic brought Miss Dooley every Tuesday
for Janice Marie's lessons. Grandpa said he'd give
his own eyes to "Three Blind Mice" if they could see
their way to disappear. Piano practice sessions drove
Aunt Mary Evelyn to serious courting—a new uncle
coming soon. When put to bed, Janice Marie's
fingers practiced on the bed quilt, stubby soldiers
marching in perfect time across neatly ordered
squares cut from outgrown shirts and dresses.

Weekdays, Grandpa snapped the evening paper,
tapped time on the chair's arm. Grandma hummed
among pots and pans, Janice Marie's fingers
practiced up and down the keys—"Bill Grogan's Goat,"
"Jingle Bells," "Auld Lang Syne." By spring there
were etudes, a scrap of Schuler, a bit of Bach.
Janice Marie loved those keys, those black notes
dancing up treble clefs, smashing sharps, fancy flats,
largo, staccato, pianissimo.

When news came of D-Day, talk of war's end,
Janice Marie played on, not believing the

background music could end. All her days had started
with Grandma's *Lord, keep our boys safe,* ended
with *Thank you, Lord, for caring for our boys.*

A toddler of two when her Daddy, the Uncles,
Cousin Earl shipped out, Janice Marie wasn't sure
about the war. She knew it was bad, sad; it sometimes
kept the soldiers, sometimes sent them to heaven.

Grandpa said, *Harry Truman will end it all.*
It's time.
Grandma nodded.
An awful bomb fell.
The world dripped silence,
and huge horror
birthed its pain.

✪

Uncle Ernest came home first, got hugged,
kissed, cried over; gave Grandpa a German knife.
Saturday morning, sleepy-eyed Janice Marie found
Uncle Owen and Cousin Earl gobbling
country ham, pouring gravy over Grandma's
biscuits. Monday, Janice Marie's daddy walked
up the sidewalk, duffle bag across his shoulder,
box under his arm. He laughed, hugged her hard,
gave her a tiny doll, Grandma a silk kimono.
We skipped the evening news, raised our glasses
to family gathered around the piano. Janice Marie
played "When Johnny Comes Marching Home."
Grandpa sang the loudest.

III. Work

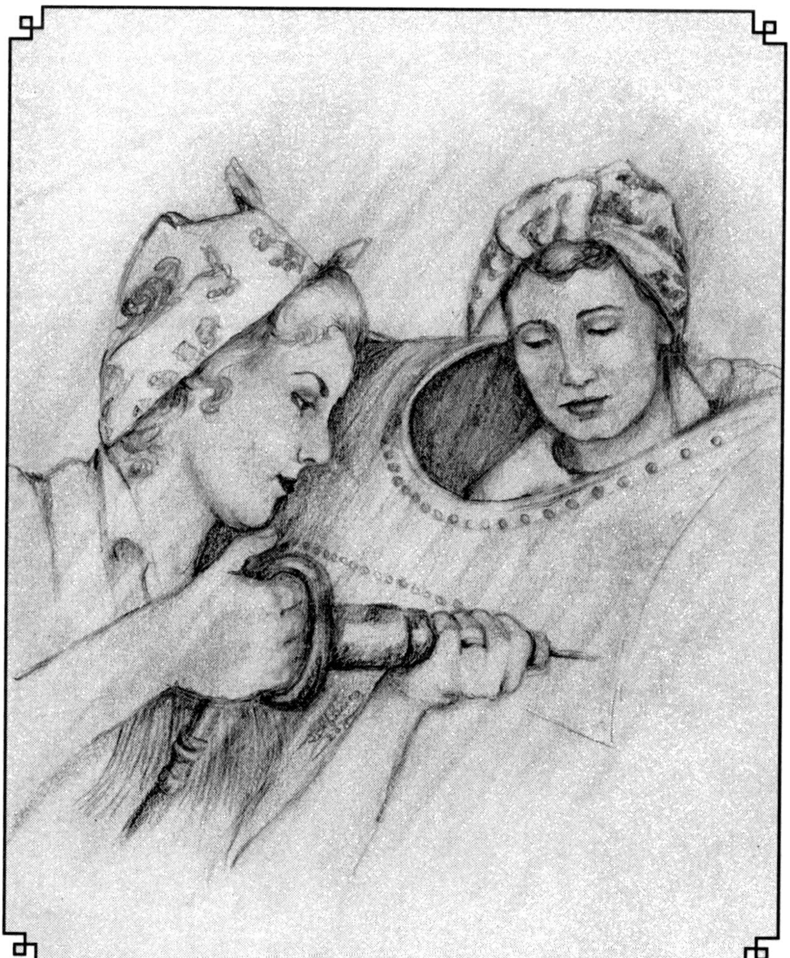

... blasting, welding, creating machines for war.

The Banker

A missed curve on a foggy mountain road
left a fine son of America a cripple, no chance
to prove the manhood never questioned at a desk
where he talked loans, interest rates, collateral, risk.

Gone long months, his brothers write of France,
foxholes, bitter cold, dead Germans. He whistles
"Yankee Doodle Dandy" under his breath,
bolstering courage unpracticed at the bank;

hopes his smile, friendly manner are enough
for the town or any critic of a man not in uniform.
As the courthouse clock chimes six,
young Edward Elkins leaves the bank. He checks

the lock, nods to Henry Oakes sweeping the sidewalk,
tips his hat to the grandpas on the square,
and tapping his leg with a rolled copy
of *The Daily Times*, limps up the street toward home.

Women Wait

Duty and country
broke a mother's heart,
though only a pillow knew her tears.
The last man to leave, the last son
of a now-barren womb walked down the road
to war with innocent ideas of bravery,
brawn spurring him to a battlefield.

We plowed and chopped, sold our
garden goods and quilts,
shushed and rocked the babes,
turned our mirrors to the wall.
Our lives filled with the sounds
women make when their men
are gone and waiting aches their hearts.

The Victory Garden

Please Mama, please Mama, stop and rest.
That ole mule's goin' to drag you down.
Hear me, Mama, please, this ain't no test,
I'm not a child, I'm strong and sound.
There's more you know, I feel it strong,
don't shut me out, don't do me wrong.

Tap it down, pat it down, tap it down,
pat it down into dirt, soft and brown.

Please Mama, please Mama, stop and rest.
All day we've sweated, plowed, and sowed;
surely you see we've done our best.
Hush son, be quiet, tend your row.
Talk can wait; plant those seeds in the ground,
so we're done 'fore the sun goes down.

Tap it down, pat it down, tap it down,
pat it down into dirt, soft and brown.

He marks the row, seeds drop one by one,
but a heavy heart spoke his need:
Mama, I'm near a man, I'm your son,
all that's left. Is there some dark deed
you're keepin' hid? If it's nothin' good,
just tell me, Mama, like you should.

Tap it down, pat it down, tap it down,
pat it down into dirt, soft and brown.

Her head bent low, weary shoulders bowed,
swift, silent tears fall down and down.
She reins in the mule, stops the plow,
straightens her back, then turns around.
She faces this son, so near a man,
sees fear in his eyes, takes his hands.

Tap it down, pat it down, tap it down,
pat it down into dirt, soft and brown.

She understands his anxious need
and hopes he's able to share the weight
of what she's known for lonely weeks.
Now on a day grown dark and late,
she tells him of crosses row on row,
gleaming in sun, rain, moon, or snow.

The man she loved, his father brave,
is now at peace in a hero's grave.

Tap it down, pat it down, tap it down,
pat it down into dirt, soft and brown.

Me and Baby Ralph

Harry and me lived in a nice duplex
on Chambers Avenue, paid for furniture
with part of my check from Woolworth's.
I worked up to the month the baby came.
My boss, Mrs. Wright, was kind
and understanding. She stood up
for me to Mr. Findley, the manager.

She offered to let me stay with her,
but Mama thinks her little apartment
isn't up to our standards—whatever that means.
I like Mrs. Wright, and sometimes I
think of packing our things and walking
the six blocks to her place, not telling
anyone until it's done.

Harry's never seen little Ralph. He says
in his last letter to be patient. It won't be
long until he's home, things will be different.
Daddy claims Harry doesn't know what he's
talking about. He says the Japs are fierce
in the Pacific, Europe is still a bloody mess,
and only God knows what will happen next.

I sit in this porch swing, nursing my baby
boy, wondering what I'll do if Harry
doesn't come back from the war. How would
I make it on my own? I try to be grateful for all
the help Mama and Daddy give us, but they
treat me like a child, and little Ralph
as if he's theirs, not mine.

Precious Memories

Precious memories, how they linger
How they ever flood my soul.
In the stillness of the midnight
Precious, sacred scenes unfold.
—*J. B. Wright*

Mona Henderson stares across pews, past ladies'
Sunday hats—eyes unblinking, unseeing. She stares past
dust motes dancing in sunlight streaming through
stained glass windows, her mind held captive by distant
memories. The Clabo sisters' pure harmony fills
the church, winds ribbons of melody around

scenes washing through Mona's mind. She wanders
back to happy times before The War called her son,
her brother, two cousins, three neighbors. Eyes closed,
she breathes in a springtime past, a Sunday picnic,
singing, clapping, Paulie and Angie playing catch,
laughing with their friends.

The memories won't hold; nothing seems sacred,
secure about her life now. Paul's in New Jersey,
tries to write each week; works long hours,
blasting, welding, creating machines for war.

He last wrote:
Dear Mona, I miss you. Any word from the boy?

She answers: *Neighbor's sick again,*
Aunt Mabel fine in Kansas, no desserts at
the last church supper, shutter came loose,
Angie held the ladder while I fixed it. Grandpa
helped with the weeding, we planted
the rest of the corn, picked the last of the peas.

Do you think there'll be seed for a fall garden
this year? The scrap metal cart came by again;
I gave them the broken shovel, some cans
I saved, a few bent nails, rusty bolts.
I'm doing okay, and I miss you, too.
No word from Paulie.

Joppa Mountain Blues

A grandfather's lament upon his grandson's going to war

I did my part in the first Great War;
those bloody cries still haunt my dreams.
I thought we settled the German score,
but they're back much worse, it seems.

While bloody screams still haunt my dreams,
a German evil encroaches;
they're back much worse it seems,
as the midnight hour approaches.

A German evil encroaches
upon the youth we've sent to war,
and the midnight hour approaches
when slaughter comes as ne'er before

upon the youth we've sent to war
from safety here on the mountain,
to slaughter none have seen before
where death is always certain.

Our safety here on the mountain
feels sad and strange at times
since life and death seem certain
to give and take in kind.

We feel sad and strange at times.
I thought we settled the German score;
we gave and took in kind.
I *did* my part in the first Great War.

Strangers Among Us, 1944

A midnight train stopped overlong, shadowed
shapes shuffled onto trucks rumbling off into
the night, yellow beams aimed toward river-bottom farms.

Like The War, winter lingered, left sodden
turf underfoot; food was rationed, children
whined, a hungry wildcat prowled close to town.
Spring could not break winter's clutch. No prayers
or children's wishes brought forth blooms
on bare, brittle branches in a town gray
with despair and hopeless news from the front.

Rumors swelled like creeks, spread through
town, seeped through keyholes into ears
thought deaf to surprise. Nervous hands dialed
neighbors, unanswered questions rang across lines,
created phantoms. Monstrous fears filled the vacuum
meant for spring. Schoolyards fell quiet—
Sunday sermons couldn't quell the dread.

Noises rose from the rich river farms, motors
hummed, tools clanked, men's voices drifted
over heavy clods of fresh-turned earth. Curious
boys—self-appointed spies—pursued rumor, braved
the dark country road, crept close, scurried home
with specter tales stretched into a message tainted
by their foolish love affair with war.

Facts emerged: innocent fields harbored terror
as foreign hands wielded farm tools, not weapons
of war. Field glasses showed fair heads, strong backs
bent to tasks done well with hands purpled by cold
river wind. Granddad heard language unknown,
yet understood. His fireside tales stirred more questions.

Good Friday morning found Helga Gernst trudging muddy ruts to farm field edges. Cupped ear strained toward men marking furrowed rows, tears streamed her face as voices of homeland rose on fog-laden air. We bowed to her sobbing cries: *Oh, this awful war. Those boys have broken-hearted mamas, too.*

Moving to Secret City

We loaded our pickup trucks
with kids, hope, and bought-on-time
furniture, and wearing Sunday duds,
took off for hills beyond Knoxville.
Mystery jobs waited for trustworthy folks
from all over. Word went out fast,
"Call the man, they're hiring now."
Lots of questions—most passed the test.
Honor's big where we're from.

The notice said they needed carpenters,
plumbers, electricians, cement finishers,
teachers, typists, welders, brick masons.
Granddaddy Jenkins worried no one
would stay to run the town
but him and the rocking-chair boys
at Joe Parker's General Store.
The wives said they'd always
run the town anyway.

Beverly and Wanda took the Trailways
for promised jobs needing nimble hands,
quick minds. High school diplomas
safe in suitcases, typing certificates too.
"Don't worry, Momma, Daddy,
we'll be fine, we'll write."
Apartments shared with girls
from Kansas, Ohio, Georgia;
cute boys to date, dancing on Fridays.
Grown-up times for working girls.

Whispers ran around road curves,
over telephone wires.
Scientists working night and day:
hush-hush stuff—none knew what.
All those hired
took an oath not to tell.
It's for our country, the war, said some;
others, not so sure.
Maybe new weapons?
Something big to end the war?
Yeah, something big.

The Foreman Talks to Joe on V-J Day

Okay, so the plant might close soon.
What you need, Joe, is a sense
of real appreciation
for what's happening now.
Come on, get off your stupid
self-pity, join the street crowds;
sing, shout, kiss a pretty girl,
stomp your feet on ration books,
meatless dinners, past hard times.

Of course we're proud of our crews,
tough men, women, long hours,
no complaints. We were a team,
all for one, one for all. We never missed
a deadline. We were the best.
But it was a war, Joe, a goddamn
war that lasted way too long.
Who knows, Joe, they may retool
and keep some of us working.

Come on, Joe, let's join
the street parade, celebrate.
There's good times ahead.

IV. Youth and Innocence

longs for summer, freedom
from chalk dust, oiled floors...

Dream Skate, 1944

Out the door in sock feet; no one pays her
any mind. Key secure on a string necklace,
shiny skates ready to fly. She crosses the yard,
a last glance toward the silent house. Stops
at the sidewalk, quietly closes the gate.

Whistling softly between her teeth,
she bends over scraped knees, tightens skates
to scuffed, sturdy oxfords. Steadies herself
against a fence post, pushes off into the
quiet shade of the neighborhood.

She glides past hedges, lawns, closed shop doors,
notes thick Sunday papers on porches,
rounds the corner past Miss Chaney's victory garden,
wonders at the Steiner's wash on the line,
notes Paulie Brennan's bright red coupe,

dust covered, awaiting his return. Maneuvers
the bulge of sycamore roots, jumps the curb,
zooms across the alley in a one-skate sweep, passes
Holy Trinity—a pipe organ's rich chords
match rhythm with her swinging arms. Short-cuts

to the corner schoolhouse, circles deserted
playground swings. Amos Asbury's dog yaps hello.
Braking with her shoe toe, she pokes a finger through
the fence for a friendly lick. Then, six houses in a row,
silk service flags—five blue stars, one gold. Final turn

to home, the post office flag waves red, white,
blue—bright hope for peace, a war-free world.
No longer pigtailed, freckle nosed, her right hand
snaps a smart salute to the WAC she
dreams she will become.

Missing Marcus

Preston McFee glances at the schoolroom map
with casual eye, concludes the world
is mostly blue, blinks twice as the teacher points
to green and brown blobs, returns his focus
to the window framing a frigid February day.

Preston McFee sees his world an unsettled place,
filled with news of battles, wounded, dead.
He finds comfort in a soft, gray sky where
no planes roar, no bombs burst. He likes school
okay until war talk creeps into the day.

Preston McFee longs for summer, freedom
from chalk dust, oiled floors, damp wool coats,
overcooked cabbage. Summer means fishing,
baiting his hook with worms dug from Grandma's garden,
sitting on the bank, thinking of nothing, waiting for a bite.

Preston McFee thinks about big brother Marcus,
good times before the war. Lazy day
talk of batting averages, Mom's chocolate cake,
the Dodson twins getting married, Uncle Mike selling
his farm, moving to Detroit to build fighter planes.

Preston McFee walks home alone—no playing
catch, riding bikes, flying kites with Ronnie Roberts,
not since the news of his dad, a gold star in their window
now. He does not know what to say, which words won't
jinx his brother, won't make him die.

Preston McFee believes in magic, casting spells, looks
for signs, carries a rabbit's foot, lucky arrowhead, says
double prayers, touches a special rock and chants Marcus's
name. He repeats the ritual often, his boy heart
aching to believe it will bring his brother home.

Sixth Grade Friends

Sara Tischner's father sings
opera. I didn't know what it was.
I rode my bike up the alley, hid
behind their garage, listening.

Sara found me, and now we
are friends. She told me
the foreign words tell sad
stories for the magical music.

Mr. Tischner is a tenor
and famous in cities where
they like opera. He travels
long distances to sing.

Jacob, Sara's big brother,
is an army captain in France.
Sara says when she grows up
she will write an opera

about our brave soldiers in
the war. After the sad parts,
the ending music will be happy
because we will win.

Will Teddy and Wayne Ever Know?

What does your town think about the *war?*
I heard a reporter ask Mr. McCallie
at the hardware store.

A town thinks? A new idea for me,
my thoughts so different from Wayne's, Teddy's,
their bedroom now Mama's private chapel.

We'll get those Japs, Wayne laughed, pounded
Teddy's back. *I want to notch my gun with
a dozen Krauts.* Teddy grinned.

I think this war is horrid, Hitler a monster from hell.
We've no word from my brothers for weeks;
Mama kneels by their beds, prays.

*Well, sir, our town is behind our boys one hundred
percent,* Mr. McCallie tells the reporter,
satisfied smiles on both their faces.

Lost on Joppa Mountain

I had to leave, get away from tears,
hugs—big brother Jeremy home on leave,
the family hero. No war for me, no medals,
no enemies destroyed, no taste of victory.
—Zeke, the son who stayed at home

He flees the farmhouse in a dead run.
The wind grabs strangled anger as he crosses
the meadow; heavy boots crush tall, brown grass.
Long strides slow when he reaches the first trees.
Grasping underbrush, low limbs, he begins to climb.

The Mountain shifts, feels the presence of the boy-man,
old friend to craggy coves, wind wisdom, solitude.

Ancient limestone looms cold under gnarled trees;
their black limbs reach toward the white winter sky.
He stumbles over tangled vines, wicked briars tearing
cloth, skin. He rails against the burning rage that stabs
love so long in place, thought safe from all.

Stormy centuries of scars hide under mossy stones,
sodden leaves, twisting roots. The Mountain sighs.

He's missed the old path, the trail he and Jeremy
first marked tracking deer, hunting squirrels;
daring boys chased shadows, imagined ghosts.
Lost, weary of body, heart, he struggles against
the dwindling light, the dark place in his heart.

From deep within Earth, energies of the Mystery
emerge, move into the dusk. The Mountain listens.

Mind frayed, body numb, he crawls onto a craggy
ledge, peers into the valley below. An upward draft
carries reminders of dinnertime. He spies the windows
of his mother's kitchen, aches for family,
good times before the war.

Evensong rides the breeze through scrubby pines,
an owl swoops low, wings toward the meadow;
in deep quiet, the Mountain waits.

Grenade

A newsreel at the Roxy
showed our boys brave and determined,
guns and bayonets poised, pride in every move.

A close-up showed a grenade, a word
reminding me of cool drinks in summer shade.
I later learned the word was from a fruit.

A soldier held one out, all ridges and lines;
it did resemble a peculiar pineapple.

He pulled out a pin,
tossed the grenade onto a big hill of dirt
that disappeared in black noise.

Schoolroom Questions

The window glass is foggy,
but I can see the trees bending
in the winter blast. Mrs. Nichols' voice
drones on about studying Europe
for more than war.

All my uncles—Davy, Chester, Martin
—are in the war. My mom explained they
are also brothers, sons, husbands,
but all I know is my uncles are gone,
maybe not coming home,

could get wounded, hurt bad like
Jimmy, our preacher's boy who walks
with a crutch, his one leg hopping along.
Teacher pulls down a map, and it hits me
that the world is mostly

water, but we only talk about
the land. Seems strange the world's blue
with water, 'n maps divide land
up in pink, blue, green patches. I know they
are countries and states,

but pink's a sissy color for any
country. Even if they are your enemy
now, they could be your friend later. Like
when I got in a fight with Kenny, then
we made up and played

ball the next day. I'm tired of the war
and my uncles being gone, Momma
and Daddy always worried, no good cakes
or fun stuff to eat. I don't know
any Japs or Germans except

Hans Weisman's granny talks German
sometimes, but Daddy says she's a good
American and the best cook in Lincoln
County for sure. Anyway, I think they
could all just quit fighting and shake hands,

and maybe make ball teams and get along
with each other. This war and killing
people 'cause they go to a church
with a funny name and meet on Saturday
is 'bout the stupidest thing

I ever heard of in my whole life.
Sometimes you just can't figure out what
makes grown-ups do these crazy things.
And I don't buy that "you'll
understand when you're older"

thing Mrs. Nichols said when I asked
her about it. I was only five when
my uncles left, and I'm in fourth grade
now. That's a whole lot older,
and I still don't understand it.

Night Watch

The child woke, unafraid.
She lay still, blinking in the dark,
listening, red curls a silhouette against
the white featherbed.
The old house, quiet beyond
Grandpa's snauzzz-snauzzz snores.
Something else, something different
coaxed her from the high bed.
Tiny feet, cold against linoleum,
padded silently to find Grandpa alone
in the big four-poster. Ignoring
the chill creeping up her legs,
she pushed the heavy door,
stepped into the cool April night.

The slow clitch-a-clitch,
clitch-a-clitch of a porch
rocker, her grandmother
wrapped in faded pink chenille.
"What are you doing awake?
Come here, child."
Eager little body nestled, settled.
Clitch-a-clitch, clitch-a-clitch.
From near the creek, a counter-melody
of pure, clear notes repeated
across the night.
What's that, Grandma?
Is that a bird?

"That's Whippoorwill, honey."
Clitch-a-clitch, clitch-a-clitch.
Whip-poor-will, whip-poor-will.
What's he saying?
Why's he singing in the dark?
"Why, he's a night watcher,
taking care that all is safe until
morning. He's like a beacon
of sound, telling everyone he's
there, watching, paying attention."
Is that what you're doing, Grandma?
Are you a night watcher?
Clitch-a-clitch, clitch-a-clitch.
"Let's sing back to him. He'll
know we're watching, too."

Girlfriends

When our boyfriends enlisted,
we were excited, proud. Then
reality set in; it was possible they
might never come back. Our town
seemed so strange with so many
women without men by their sides.
Silent, stunned, we never seemed
to know what to do with ourselves.

We girlfriends have sweethearts,
brothers, cousins fighting in Europe,
stories of frozen mud, bleeding feet
in foxholes. Bombs falling, grenades
exploding, always danger. Some are sailors
in the Pacific; we hear of boats sinking
in dark ocean waters—would anyone
ever find them?

The President spoke on the radio
about how we were *all in this*
together, and we felt proud and
inspired. We got busy doing our part.

We gals are never idle now; we pile
scrap metal by the curb, collect
newspapers, roll bandages, save
our sugar rations to make cookies
for the USO boys. Many write letters
to brothers, husbands, sweethearts,
neighbor boys, and especially
to the guys who have no kin.

The wounded soldiers in our hospital love for us to read to them, write their letters, or simply sit beside their beds and talk, maybe sing a special song.

Main Street Blues, 1942

Maizie and Beth stride Main Street arm in arm,
heads bent in whispered secrets—fragile armor
for girls deprived of youthful hopes.
No sweethearts' Friday paychecks to promise

sodas, jukebox dances. No Saturday doorbell
announces spicy whiffs of aftershave,
shivers of romance for young women's dreams.
They know Friday's whistle,

a respite from factory hours, acrid smells
of war machines. They know stories old men
tell around the courthouse square,
battle tales of another Great War.

Maizie and Beth find solace in five-cent sodas,
read drugstore magazines, smooth them back
to the shelf. They ride bicycle trails, spread sparse
picnics, spend lazy hours reading pulp stories

of betrayal, love, loss—their novel escape
from strife-laden lives. Maizie and Beth stride
Main Street, their Saturday smiles feigning faith
in a future bright with hope. They hurry

to the Bijou, lose their hearts to Rhett
and Scarlett, a drama of bygone battles,
and for an afternoon, two young women forget
the war, loneliness, and loss.

Facing the Folks

They think I'm still at Stonehill,
a boarding house for girls.
I joined the WACs last Friday,
I'm thrilled at last to serve.

My folks are fine, good people
I never think to blame,
but *their* plan sees my future
safe with a married name.

I know I have to tell them;
perhaps they'll understand
I've a right to live my dream
as much as any man.

When Bobby joined the Marines
in December forty-one,
Ma and Pa were very proud,
no protests, no, not one.

They sent him off with kisses,
their hero off to war.
My only hope and wish is for
their blessing, nothing more.

LEGACY

Isabel sits in the shade of the maple tree
Great Granddad Ryan planted when he bought
this land a century ago. The iron mower
she pushed all morning left wilted green blades
for the chickens to snatch. Her clear gaze
rests on Mama's flower garden near the porch,
plump with broad hosta leaves, wavy fern fronds,
money-plant seed coins moving with the breeze.
Lavender blooms bend over the flagstones,
nod to the lemon balm across the walk.

I snap this lovely photo for my memory album,
add the sounds of birdsong coming from the woods,
chattering squirrels scrambling limb to limb,
the soft rustle of leaves as a breeze brushes by.
My eye clicks on doves, blue jays, grackles
bobbing for the cracked corn left by the hens.
A blade of wild grass, its seed pod full,
holds firm while a yellow finch pecks it clean.
A hawk circles overhead, red tail a warning flag
to scurrying life below.

As I will this picture to memory, it spills
into my heart, washes me with tranquil
gratitude. Yet Isabel's heart weighs heavy
from secret sobbing, anguished night prayers
carried down our bedroom hall, winging
with a mother's hope through the ethers
to the battlefield where her son fights for his
country—this land, his home, family,
pretty sweetheart—and perhaps dreams
of his grandmother's peaceful garden.

I Shall Not Think of War Today

With thoughts of
Emily Dickinson
and Scarlett O'Hara

I shall not think of war today,
it will not cross my mind.
There'll be no conjured images
of death of any kind.

I shall not think of war today,
instead I'll dream of birds
and other things that fly about
and mingle without words.

I shall not think of war today,
no matter what may come
by postman's hand or telegram
or neighbor's sickly son.

I shall not think of war today,
despise me if you will,
for thoughts of war and other crimes
seek more than men to kill.

I shall not think of war today,
I can't be coaxed or shamed
to do the bidding of the town,
wear widow's weeds—be blamed.

So while I think of other things
un-war-like, pure, and free,
please don't speak of death just yet;
it's not caught up with me.

Radio Songs

Radio music keeps me going.
I hear a dreamy song that promises
I'LL BE SEEING YOU and hope my
Tommy thinks of me that way too.

When Dinah Shore sings I'LL WALK
ALONE, the mood is different,
but it still makes me think of
Tommy and me being together.

I get a happy feeling when the radio
plays Bing and the Andrews Sisters
singing DON'T FENCE ME IN.
My dad sings along, teases my mom,

I think of cowboys, sunsets, traveling
west with Tommy. Last night Peggy Lee
sang WAITING FOR THE TRAIN TO
COME IN; that's me, all right, *waiting*.

I kneel at bedtime, praying God will
bring Tommy and the others home
safely. I hear Vera Lynn sing WE'LL
MEET AGAIN, and I believe.

Edith Rogers and I saw *Casablanca*
at the Bijou; later, we cried listening
to Dooley Wilson sing AS TIME
GOES BY. It was just too sad.

Late last night THAT OLD BLACK MAGIC
scattered its spell with Glenn Miller,
Skip Nelson, and the Modernaires.
If I had magic powers, I'd end this war.

Brooklyn Fire Escape, 1943

Isabella Scarparelli leans on the rail
of the fire escape, watching the stickball
game in the street below. She fingers

rosary beads with hands rough
from kneading dough at Garbarino's Bakery.
She prays more since Tony left,

her sweetheart since juinior high; they've
talked marriage for a year.
Holding hands at the movies, cuddling

on the sofa, talking about good jobs,
an apartment on Maple Street, furniture
from Mr. Horowitz's secondhand store, maybe

a car someday—it all seems an impossible
dream now, a dream Isabella
barely remembers.

Father Rosario talks of "our boys serving God
and country" at every mass now. He looks
at her and Mrs. Petrone when he says, *on land*

and sea, maybe 'cause Tony's in the Navy.
Tony loves the sea—fishing, sailing. Sometimes
he gets hired as deck hand on fishing scows

or posh sailboats off Long Island.
Isabella isn't all that crazy about water,
can barely swim, but she never says anything

to hurt Tony's feelings. Especially now, him
being on a big ship, dodging torpedoes and bullets,
risking his life for America every single day.

One Word

One word frees us of all the weight
and pain of life: That word is love.
—Sophocles (496-406 BC)

You march away, brass and percussion
ring in your ears, passion heats
your heart. Innocent eyes gleam patriot
love, muscles twitch toward exotic weapons
firing to the cheers of comrades
in arms, soldiers one and all.

You shout: *We shall never fall!*

I plod a lonely path, seek solace
in a dove's divine coo, beseech
bowed willows to buoy my sinking
soul, bargain any sliver of sunlight
to melt my glacial fear.

I surrender beneath a stoic oak
bearing witness to our love
by letters carved within a heart.

V. Faith and Hope

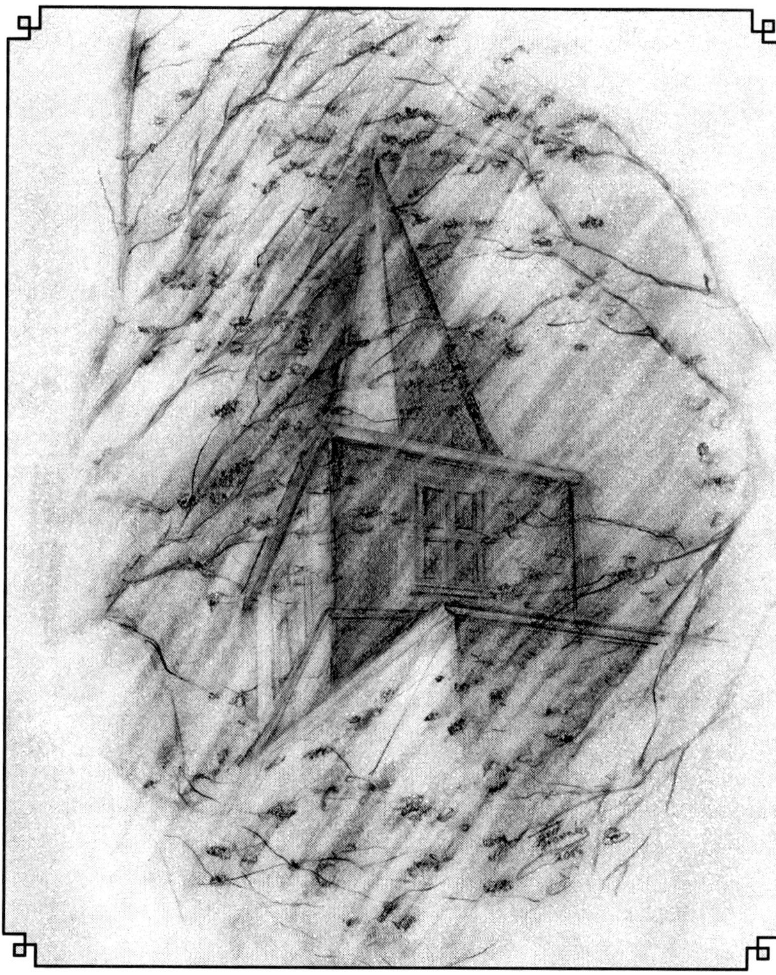

faith flowed across continents...

Dancing the Dream, 1943

The birds—terns, gulls, pelicans—
search my lacy hem for morsels left by the sea;
lonely wives walk by, sad eyes watch my
sand-stepping twirl. Memories circle

my waist in a courtship dance, strong
arms swaying, dipping—so sure, trusting
the future. Cheeks touching, arms tight,
our bodies one in dreamy beats of slow
dance tunes. Fan blades stir layers
of cigarette smoke, blue rhythms pulse
heartbeat to heartbeat, the USO
band keeping time 'til dawn.

Dream-killer, knife-edged smile
walks through our plans. Commander eyes
ablaze, he taps a strong young shoulder,
demands a different dance—a tune called
duty. Battle-dressed in flared navy trousers,
white trimmed collar frames your brave smile.
Darling, it's only for a few months—silly lie;
the same words bought our mother's trust

in my brother's clear eyes—uniformed service
she struggled to understand. No word
since his ship left port, forging over this same sea,
churning courage with every white-capped
hope of sweet victory, a hero's return. Oh, fickle
love, your untamed depths speak wild disdain
of time, any passage other than tides, winds;
you hold me in your mystery, pull me

toward tomorrow's sunrise, ever
returning to this shore where I dance
the dream, breathe in your briny promise
to bring him home.

The Quilter

Annalee Martin would not be swayed by the women
of the Thursday Quilting Circle. Needles flew as knees
touched under the great wood table in the back room
of McKenzie's Dry Goods. The striped, plaid, solid swirls

of quilting squares testified to grade-school dresses,
brothers' shirts outgrown by boys in muddy
trenches bordering millet fields in France.
Annalee refused to complain, cry, argue, or venture

into pity about The War, soldiers, generals, politics,
or any sermon Pastor Harwood fired off from
the Methodist pulpit. She hummed songs from the radio,
kept her hair brushed and curled, red lipstick shining,

wrists dabbed with Evening in Paris.
Nothing dowdy or sad about Annalee.
She spoke of lovely weather, a delicious apple,
a stranger's kind word, the bumper crop

of beans canned in July, her mother's improved health,
her daughter's new job, the upcoming county fair,
and who might win the ribbon for best peach pie.
She thrived on make-do ideas that eased the pain

borne by the busy bees buzzing 'round the quilting
table. She teased memories: days, nights
when evening news quoted the local mayor,
spoke of farm prices, visiting musicians—peaceful news.

Annalee wore a gold locket holding Scottie Martin's
smiling face. She willed him safely home. Her strong thread
of faith flowed across continents, oceans for him
to grasp and follow back to his mother's love.

Church Pew, 1942

After the news article, once empty
Sundays filled with warm
attention. Folks patted my hand,
proud of your bravery, patriotism.

News came about Billy Wallace,
then the Johnson boys, all lost—
Maggie Johnson's screams echoed
down three valleys.

Everyone's quiet about it;
no direct looks,
only passing mumbles,
a tight lift to the corners of mouths.

I tell myself you're safe,
braver, smarter than the rest.
The pew beside me empty
only a short while before I'll hear

your sweet voice lifted to the strains
of *Amazing Grace*.

My Wanting Heart

I'll be seeing you in all the old familiar places
That this heart of mine embraces, all day through.
—Irving Kahal / Sammy Fain

Mourners filled the church.
The Reverend praised goodness
of brave young men.
Your mother sobbed;
Dad and Brother never left her side.

When my loneliness seems an endless
pain, park trails beckon. I step off
memories of high school giggles,
summer hayrides, first kisses, first love,
plans for our life, plans for always.

Goodbye kisses at the train station,
a last touch, a deep gaze, a whispered love.
I sense your nearness now, feel your love,
pour this moment of memory
into my wanting heart.

The Newport Train Station, 1943

Squat and red, it sat behind
the courthouse, roof tiles marked
with rust, soot. Folks hung around
waiting for a troop train's slow
grind through town. When soldiers
leaned out windows to kiss the girls,
school boys slapped their caps against
their legs, whooped and yelled.

Methodist ladies handed up baskets
of home-baked cookies, Bibles,
magazines, knitted wool socks.
Janie Archer ran alongside
every troop train, waving her arms,
shouting over and over,
Have you seen my soldier?
Have you seen Jeremiah Archer?
Please, tell me, have you seen him?
until the caboose disappeared,
leaving us all behind.

The Witness Tree

Dearest Robert, do you feel
the warm passion of my love
surging across blood-drenched fields?
No bullet or bomb can divert the intent
of my heart to yours. My love pillows
your dreams, erases your fears.
Do you recall our walks
by Miller's Church, sunlight streaming
through the leaves, the kisses I gave
to keep you safe until you returned?
Under those ancient branches,
we embraced, vowed our love.

Today I touched that gnarled old tree.
Dear Robert, I rubbed the rough bark,
sent kisses to build an armor of love
until you come back to me. I wore your
wool coat, hugged it to me, pretended
we were walking hand in hand.
Darling man, when you come home
to me, we'll walk this path. You'll
wear this coat, and I'll hold your arm,
rub my cheek on this soft, warm sleeve,
and once again we'll kiss, grateful
to renew our love under the witness tree.

They Played "The Blue Danube"

on the radio
this morning, and I
waltzed around the kitchen,
imagined your arms
around me,
your cheek on mine.

I remember
the time we danced
right out of the school gym,
stumbled into parked cars;
you leaned me against
Mr. Weaver's Packard,
gave me a wicked kiss.

I remember
Kate Sawyer's wedding—
the band played all
our favorites.
We danced every dance
hoping the music
would never end.

I remember
we turned up the car radio
on the River Road,
danced in the grass
while the moon made
silver magic on
the water.

They played "The Blue Danube"
on the radio
this morning, and I
waltzed around the kitchen—
felt your arms around me,
held your memory
in my heart.

Evensong

When she drew the bow across
her cello's strings, deep sensuous notes
wrapped sultry summer evenings
like slow waves against a parched shore.

Melodies of dreams opened our ears and hearts
to joy long displaced by the sacrifice
of hard times. From the voices
of music greater than the fear of war came

the love and hope of Schroeder, Schuster,
Bach, and Paganini in scale and form known
to few but loved by all. In the gloaming's glow,
we sat on porches, stoops, and curbs letting music

birthed in hearts and minds of nations now gone
insane remind of something greater than
any evil scheme mere humans might employ.
Lillian Chaney, born plain, crippled of foot,

played her stirring solo concerts to a village
audience of every age who loved her
for the peaceful hope she brought them in
the language none would ever destroy.

Homecoming

My darling boy, you came home
to me
just as you said you would.
I'll come home, Mama. I promise I will.
You served
so bravely, made me so proud.
My hand on your fevered brow
feels foreign—not my own.
We'll celebrate a happy homecoming.

You and I, dear son,
shared the moment of your
first breath;
here, tonight, we'll share your last.
The Great Mystery
glorious at this bedside
emits the promise of a Love
even greater than ours.

My Hair Hangs Loose

On the day of war's end, we cry,
"Victory is ours!"
with tears, shouts of joy.
A united whole, peopled
from generations gone, joined
in allied strength.

I sit on the curb, jaws sore
from smiles, watch street dances,
old, young celebrate the golden
hour of V-J Day.
My hair hangs loose,
all hairpins gone the way
of Momma's knives, Grandpa's tools,
shed door hinges melted
into war machines.

My hands, rough from chores
and factory work, seem foreign,
no longer a young girl's pride. I feel
no pang, no loss; my heart is full,
this victory ours.
There will still be days of ration books,
no new cars, no new clothes, no boys
to woo my heart away from long
months of waiting, hoping for this day.

But that is sure to change.
Victory is ours.

EXTRA! EXTRA!

The sun's hardly up, and I hear a shout,
a newsboy walking up the street
calling out to all,
"Extra! Extra! War is over!"

I struggle awake, watch the curtains switch
with the breeze, listen for kitchen sounds,
hoping Mama's made the coffee. I feel
a strange, new stirring as if a wild, loud
dream is trying to catch my attention
before it completely fades.

There it is again: "Extra! Extra!"
How can that be? A newsboy shouting—
never before, never before, then it *must* be...
My bare feet don't mind the cold floorboards
or the wet grass or the rough gravel.
Here, boy, here, give me a paper;
keep the change.

Judith Duvall has been passionate about writing since producing her first poem, a masterpiece in crayon, at age four. Her poetry has appeared in two anthologies from the Knoxville Writers' Guild poetry groups: *Bleeding Hearts* and *Familiar Landscapes,* published by Tellico Books. Duvall's work also appears in MOTIF Vol.3*: All the Livelong Day* and *Kudzu Literary Journal.* Her poem "In the Presence of Trees" won second place in *Kudzu*'s 2010 national poetry competition. Her fiction has been included in three anthologies by Greyhound Books and in the 2012 Knoxville Writers' Guild anthology, *A Tapestry of Voices.*

A graduate of the University of Tennessee, Duvall currently lives near English Mountain and the shores of Douglas Lake in Jefferson County, Tennessee.

CPSIA information can be obtained
at www.ICGtesting.com
Printed in the USA
FFOW04n1929310816
27283FF

9 781604 542387